ISBN 978-1-998317-65-3

Cover illustration and design by Charlotte Chang with the aid of artificial intelligence.

First Edition: January, 2025

Ai Wowo

A little boy in Beijing loved sweet treats, so his mom made him soft, sticky rice balls with yummy red bean filling.

艾窝窝 · ài wō wō

Sticky Rice Ball

1

Bingtang Hulu

A little boy in Beijing loved sweet treats, so his mom made him soft, sticky rice balls with yummy red bean filling.

冰糖葫芦
bīng táng hú lú

Hawthorn Skewer

2

Chunjuan

During springtime, families rolled up veggies and meat in crispy wrappers to make a snack full of fun and flavor.

春卷 (chūn juàn)

Spring Roll

Dousha Bao

A little girl loved sweet red beans so much that her grandma hid them inside fluffy steamed buns just for her.

dòu shā bāo
豆沙包

Red Bean Bun

4

E Dan Bing

A farmer's family cooked thin, soft goose egg pancakes for breakfast, and they were so good they made them every morning.

é dàn bǐng
鹅蛋饼

Goose Egg Pancake

5

Fengli Su

A baker made sweet little pineapple pastries for his kids, and they couldn't stop smiling after the first bite.

Guihua Gao

Kids picked tiny yellow flowers to help their mom make sweet, soft cakes that smelled as lovely as they tasted.

guì huā gāo
桂花糕

Osmanthus Cake

Hongshao Rou

A chef cooked pork belly in a sweet sauce for hours, and when kids tried it, they said, "This is the best meat ever!"

hóng shāo ròu
红烧肉

Braised Pork Belly

Jiaozi

A family made tiny dough pockets filled with meat and veggies, and they loved eating them together during festivals.

jiǎo zǐ
饺子

Dumpling

9

Kaoya

A chef roasted a duck until the skin was golden and crispy, and it became a favorite for family feasts.

烤鸭
kǎo yā

Roast Duck

10

Laozao

A mom made warm, sweet fermented rice soup for her little boy on a cold day, and he loved the soft rice grains and gentle sweetness.

láo zāo
醪糟

Sweet Fermented Rice Soup

Mahua

A grandma twisted dough into fun shapes, fried it, and turned it into a crunchy treat for her grandkids

má huā
麻花

Fried Dough Twist

12

Niurou Mian

A chef made warm noodle soup with beef for a boy who was cold, and the boy said it was the best soup ever!

niú ròu miàn
牛肉面

Beef Noodle Soup

Oufen

A mom cooked this sweet, warm lotus root soup to keep her kids cozy on chilly nights.

藕粉 (ǒu fěn)

Lotus Root Starch Soup

14

Pidan Shourou Zhou

A mom made rice porridge with soft pork and preserved eggs to cheer up her sick little boy.

Qingtuan

Kids helped shape green sticky rice balls made green by the juice of fresh grasses, and their reward was the sweet surprise inside!

qīng tuán
青团

Green Sticky Rice Ball

16

Roujiamo

A baker stuffed juicy meat inside a warm bun, making the perfect sandwich for kids to enjoy.

ròu jiā mó
肉夹馍

Chinese Hamburger

17

Shaomai

A family made little dumplings with open tops, filled with rice and meat, and shared them during a feast.

烧麦 (shāo mài)

Siu Mai

18

Tangyuan

A grandma rolled sticky rice balls with sweet fillings, and her family loved eating them together at festivals.

tāng yuán
汤圆

Sweet Rice Ball

19

Wotou

A farmer baked these little corn buns for his kids, and they enjoyed their simple, slightly sweet taste.

窝头 (wō tóu)

Steamed Corn Bun

20

Xiaolongbao

A family carefully steamed soup dumplings, and kids had so much fun eating them without spilling the soup inside.

xiǎo lóng bāo
小笼包

Soup Dumplings

21

Yuebing

At the Mid-Autumn Festival, kids opened these mooncakes to find sweet surprises like lotus or bean paste inside.

yuè bǐng
月饼

Mooncake

22

Zongzi

During Dragon Boat Festival, kids helped wrap sticky rice dumplings in bamboo leaves, making it a fun family tradition.

zòng zǐ
粽子

Sticky Rice Dumpling

23

Guess what? There aren't any Chinese food names that start with the letters I, V, or U! Why? It's because in pinyin—the way we write Chinese words using the alphabet—words just don't start with these letters! It's like these letters decided to take a little nap while all the other letters joined the food party. So, while we can find yummy treats for almost every other letter, I, V, and U are still waiting for their turn to shine!

24

www.ingramcontent.com/pod-product-compliance
Lightning Source LLC
Chambersburg PA
CBHW041449120626
46547CB00002B/394